BORN TO WIN

BE CONFIDENT, BELIEVE IN YOU

SALLY ANN BHARAT

Published by Self Publish

Cover designed by Cover Designer

This book is intended for personal growth and development and entertainment purposes only. The author and publisher do not guarantee that anyone following these steps will be successful in life. The author and publisher shall have no liability or responsibility to anyone with respect to any loss or damage caused or alleged to be caused, directly or indirectly by information contained in this book.
This book is a work of fiction. Names, characters, places, and incidents either are products of the author's imagination or are used fictitiously. Any resemblance to actual persons, living or dead, events, or locales is entirely coincidental.

Sally Ann Bharat
Visit my website at www.johncmaxwellgroup.com/sallyannbharat

Printed in the United States of America

First Printing: November 2018
Stratosa Coaching & Consulting Ltd

ISBN: 9781790235612

Sally Ann Bharat

This book is dedicated to

All those amazing people

Who have allowed me to positively impact their lives over the years.

Thank you for your trust in me.

ACKNOWLEDGEMENTS

I would like to say thank you to:

Adrian Jones, Dolly Bharat, and Kerry Ann Simon-Singh,

Who continue to love and support me daily.

Richard and Thandiwe Roach

Who believed and had confidence in who I am and what I can achieve

And to the people who shared their ideas for this book:

Christopher Gibbons

John Harrison

Rosetta Bedeau

Nievia Ramsundar

Contents

FORETHOUGHT:

A WINNING MIND-SET, A WINNING ATTITUDE, CONFIDENCE, AND BELIEF IN YOURSELF, MAKE YOU A WINNER

"We were all born to win; but to win, we must have a winning mind-set, a winning attitude, confidence, and belief in ourselves."

– Sally Ann Bharat

*W*HY ARE SOME PEOPLE WINNERS and others are not? That question has been asked millions of times. You will hear many answers and theories.

Consider some of the popular ones:

- Winners are self-motivators
- Some people are lucky, others are not
- Education makes all the difference
- Losing results from lack of effort
- People who are afraid of losing never win

I have looked for answers to that question throughout my career. Let me tell you a story that I believe reveals the solution.

In 2017, two of my friends suffered job losses. Asha, a 40-year-old aircraft engineer, immediately thought to herself that her aviation career was over and there were no jobs to be found. She decided to become a stay-at-home mom. Andrus, who was 38 and also an aircraft engineer, thought to himself, "I am born to win, I believe in myself, and I am confident that I can secure a new job." He began looking for new opportunities. Within a couple of days, he was offered several jobs in other aviation companies across the globe.

One engineer thought her career was over, she would never secure another job, and so she became a stay-at-home mom. Let me make it clear that opting to concentrate your efforts on being a homemaker is admirable. The issue in this scenario is that Asha actually chose this path because she felt she had no other option, not because it was her heart's desire. The other engineer thought, "I was born to win, I am confident and believe in myself", and began looking at ways of finding opportunities.

The difference was that Andrus had a winning mind-set, a winning attitude, and possessed the belief and confidence in himself to secure a new job. Asha, on the other hand, had a losing mind-set, a losing attitude, and did not believe that she could obtain another job.

How do you develop confidence in yourself?

How do you believe in who you are in the midst of adversity?

How do you acquire a winning mind-set and attitude?

This book is a collection of a number of published and unpublished articles designed to assist you with overcoming challenges within and outside the workplace, and to teach you how to have the requisite confidence in yourself.

ONE

Can Women Reach The Top:

Shattering The Self-Imposed Glass Ceiling

*"It is confidence in our bodies, minds, and spirits that
allows us to keep looking for new adventures"*

-Oprah Winfrey.

THE LAST DECADE HAS WITNESSED a growing awareness of the value women contribute to the workplace, the impact they make on the organizational bottom line, and their contribution to the economy at large. Our very own leading women in Trinidad and Tobago, despite their struggles, losses and failures, are great examples: Paula-Mae Weeks, first female President; Kamla Persad-Bissessar, first female Prime Minister; Queen of Calypso MacArtha Linda Sandy-Lewis (Calypso Rose). Among others, they overcame and shattered the barriers that stood in their way.

One of the biggest barriers that hold us back as women from increasing our sphere of influence is our self-imposed glass ceiling. This ceiling is made up of the personal qualms we have about our ability to succeed and to handle the demands of leadership in the workplace.

As a young woman who has grappled with her own share of self-doubt, I know it takes continual courage to question the assumptions that underpin our actions, aspirations and conversations, and to lay our vulnerabilities on the line for a future that honors our deepest desire to make a meaningful mark in the world. And while there is no magic formula for doing this, I recommend that women should consider the following seven acts of courage designed to lead oneself and others.

Unleash Your Ambition

Lao Tzu wrote, "People are capable of more than they think." We have to think big before we can be bigger. Experience has shown that we do not aspire towards ambitions we have no talent to achieve. Likewise, the goals that inspire us are usually the ones we are innately predisposed to accomplish. While unleashing a new level of ambition can be daunting, it can also set us on a whole new trajectory that, over time, reveals new possibilities and hidden strengths and opportunities that we would never otherwise have seen.

Know Your Value

Do not stand by waiting for others to fully value your skill, expertise, time, and potential unless you do so yourself. Quite often, we allow negative self-talk to influence our way of thinking, which in turn causes us to under-estimate our skills and abilities and second-guess our potential. We take pride in selling ourselves short. Reflect for a moment and ask yourself: *how often do you meet a woman whose confidence outweighs her competence?* Probably never.

Roxanne, an administrative assistant, remarked, "I will never secure a job promotion, I am not experienced enough and I do not believe I am good enough." Roxanne at the time was pursuing her master's degree, and although she was the most experienced in her area of expertise, her limiting beliefs prevented her from realizing her value and achieving success. After being overlooked for several promotions, Roxanne began to take seriously the suggestions that those around her had offered about valuing and appreciating herself and her work more.

Do you really value yourself? Do you give yourself enough credit? Today, Roxanne feels very fortunate because the missed promotions, while painful at the time, helped her to rediscover herself and her value. The result is that she has removed all negative self-talk, changed her attitude, and become assertive and confident at work.

Don't Lead From The Crowd

"Don't follow the crowd, let the crowd follow you."
-Margaret Thatcher

When all you do is conform, all you have to offer is conformity. Former British Prime Minister Margaret Thatcher once said, "You can't lead from the crowd." You have to see yourself as a leader before anyone else will, and you have to be willing to build your own unique brand of leadership, even if at times it compels you to stand apart from the crowd. Develop the art of leading yourself, because it is the most important thing you will ever do as a leader.

Be Willing To Rock The Boat

I have learnt that when you withhold your opinion and tip-toe around sensitive issues, you limit your value. Women in this case are often loathe to say anything that might jeopardize them. Do not let your fear of rocking the boat keep you from challenging the consensus thinking. Many boats are in desperate need of rocking. Take the case of former president and CEO of Yahoo!, Marissa Mayer, who did some major boat-rocking when she took the helm at Yahoo! in 2012. While her changes were not all popular, there is no doubt that they helped turn the formerly wavering Yahoo! ship around.

Advocate For Yourself (Yes, "Good Girls" Do Ask!)

Doing a great job is vital, and being a quiet achiever is admirable. But this alone will not get you ahead: it will leave you behind, burnt out and bitter. If your management team does not know who you are or what you are capable of, then you deprive yourself of opportunities that are laid at the feet of those who are not shy in promoting their value in the right way and at the right time. Advocating for yourself is not about proving superiority or stroking a needy ego: it is about letting the people who can help you to add more value, do just that.

Refuse To Tolerate The Intolerable

"Women must not let themselves be intimidated." These words of advice from Debbie Kissire, vice chair/managing partner of Ernst & Young, echo a sentiment shared by many women who have worked their way to the top, often in male-dominated industries.

Very often, women have complained to me that they feel undervalued, overlooked, or undermined. People who want to be taken seriously, respected widely and valued fully, must be willing to stand up for themselves, teach people how they expect to be treated, and refuse to cower to those who seek to intimidate them. Remember, as Henry Cloud once said, "You get what you tolerate."

Embrace Risk As Crucial To Your Success

Maria Eitel, founding president of the Nike Foundation, stated: "Coming from a position of fear of not succeeding, losing your job, or not being admired, handicaps the potential of your career. I've never let fear of losing my job keep me from doing something I knew was the right thing to do." Taking actions that put you at risk of failure, criticism, rejection, and even of losing your job, can be scary and emotionally uncomfortable. You cannot achieve what you are capable of achieving by playing it safe in your comfort zone.

Two

What Should We Do When We Are the

Target Of Hurtful Office Rumors

"I would be true, for there are those who trust me;
I would be pure, for there are those who care;
I would be strong, for there are those who suffer;
I would be brave, for there is much to dare.
I would be friend of all--- the foe, the friendless;
I would be giving, and forget the gift;
I would be humble, for I know my weakness;
I would look up, and laugh, and love, and lift."

— **Howard A.Walter**

atie enjoyed working for her employers, until her new assistant joined the team, and her joy turned into unhappiness and discomfort. Katie found it difficult to build a rapport or establish a positive relationship with her colleague. Delegated tasks remained incomplete, and her assistant's attitude became unbearable.

A few months later, Katie discovered the reason for her colleague's behavior and the resulting lack of cooperation between them: Brent, a disgruntled employee, had decided to spread rumors at the office in an attempt to win friends and the approval of management. He began by suggesting to the new assistant that Katie, her supervisor, was lazy, had poor ethical standards, and should not be trusted.

Gossip can have devastating consequences. The reality is that when someone spreads false rumors about you, it affects your reputation and can damage both your personal life and your professional career.

If you are to navigate through the various difficulties caused by office rumors, you must master the art of emotional intelligence. Consider the following strategies.

Regulating Negative Emotions

Take a moment to step back from the situation. Allowing yourself to respond with feelings of horror, anxiety, anger, or even helplessness when confronted with negative gossip, can create an atmosphere of unwarranted stress or cause you to lose motivation. Use the calming strategies that work best for you: breathing, mindfulness, unplugging from work, working out, or taking walks. Giving yourself time to cool off will help you to develop constructive solutions to address the problem.

Expand Your Perspective

Negative situations can cause you to feel powerless and to lose sight of the big picture. You can feel angry, depressed, or ashamed. That is when stepping back becomes critical; reminding yourself that you were born to win and that you are an overcomer becomes key to moving forward.

It is equally important to determine what success means to you. Does it mean regaining that feeling of power and confidence? Or does it mean winning? Research has shown that negative emotions are associated with a narrower perspective and a tendency toward self-absorption – in other words, your perception is skewed. A constructive solution requires you to snap out of a negative mind-set.

Practice Self-Compassion And Even Forgiveness

During these moments, forgiveness can seem far-fetched, but cultivating forgiveness and compassion can be highly effective. It can assist you in moving forward and improving your health and well-being.

Detach Yourself From The Situation

Recognize that the situation is not a reflection on you; this behavior is not about you. It is actually the behavior of someone who is nervous and anxious about their own position within the organization. People lash out, gossip and snipe at others to protect their fragile egos. They tear you down to make themselves look slightly better by comparison.

Consider How To Respond

It becomes essential to disengage from the situation and regulate your emotions. To win the lead gossiper's sympathies, you can approach them in a sympathetic, non-confrontational way. At this stage, you will want to communicate with the person from a place that is cool and collected.

Give It Time

As the victim, your reputation across the organization and amongst others can be sabotaged and tarnished in the short or long term. Allow yourself to operate and perform your duties with high integrity and let your actions speak for you. Time is on your side.

Focus On What Is Going Right

What we feed our mind is often what our mind will cling to, so feeding our mind positive things, even in the midst of a negative situation, can be helpful in taking us to the next level. Do not allow negative situations to prevent you from enjoying what you do at work or appreciating your organization's values or benefits.

Remember That You Are Not Alone

During difficult experiences such as this, you can often feel a sense of being on your own. However, there may be other people in your organization who are experiencing something similar, so you are probably not alone. Always remember that, although it is difficult to be the subject of a negative rumor (particularly one that has no basis in reality), you cannot always control what other people say about you. But you can control how you respond, and you can be resilient.

THE PRICE TAG OF PERSONAL AND PROFESSIONAL SUCCESS:

EMOTIONAL INTELLIGENCE

"We cannot tell what situations may come upon us in the strange medley of life. But we have a choice – we can choose to control what happens in us – how we react to triggers or we can make an excuse. Your choice will determine what really counts in the end"

-Sally Ann Bharat

$\mathcal{D}$aniel Goleman said, "If your emotional abilities aren't in hand, if you don't have self-awareness, if you are not able to manage your distressing emotions, if you can't have empathy and have effective relationships, then no matter how smart you are, you are not going to get very far." That is true not just in your professional life but also in your personal life. Winners practice emotional intelligence in every aspect of their life. Emotional intelligence comes before achieving success.   It is the price tag of personal and professional success.

When I was in university, I studied Business Administration. One of the terms in business was emotional intelligence. I think this term gave great insights into what someone needs in order to achieve success personally and professionally. The term means *"a form of social intelligence that involves the ability to monitor one's own and others' feelings and emotions, to discriminate among them, and to use this information to guide one's thinking and action"*. It describes an emotional self-assessment and social emotional drivers, people must be aware of in order to have self-control and social skills that will bring them success.   That's critical because I need to firstly understand my emotions and be empathetic towards emotional social drivers before I can lead us towards achieving success.

As people, one of our greatest challenge in our personal and professional life is emotional self-awareness. We can't expect to be aware of other people emotional triggers if we are unaware of our own emotional triggers. We must understand what factors trigger our emotions before we can understand other people's emotional triggers.   Many highly gifted professionals have fallen short of success because they were not willing to pay the price. They tried to focus on building skills in various other areas only to find that having all the skills and no emotional intelligence will not help you achieve success in the long run.

Emotional SELF-AWARENESS MAKES PERSONAL AND PROFESSIONAL UPHILL CLIMB POSSIBLE

The truth you need to be aware of, not just for your professional life, but for all aspects of your life. For the last couple years or so, I have been studying emotional intelligence within one's personal and professional life. Ready? Here it is. Emotional Self-Awareness and Self-Management leads to overall Success.

Now that you have thought about it, you are probably saying, "It all makes perfect sense. Okay. So how do I begin?" But I want you to stop for a minute and reflect on it. Emotional Self-Awareness and Self-Management leads to overall success. The word emotional is inclusive. Pair that with Self Awareness – the things that make you angry, excited, fearful, disgust or surprised. So when you think about that, it's very significant. Everything in life that triggers your emotions, is uphill, meaning emotions can be challenging.

As people, our greatest challenge personally and professionally is having emotional self-awareness and self-management

EMOTIONAL – SELF AWARENESS ENABLES YOU TO ACHIEVE SUCCESS

If I were to ask you, "Do you want to be in control of your emotions?" of course your answer would be yes. The question isn't if you want it to happen. The question is how do you make it happen? The answer is by having an awareness your emotions, your triggers and their impact. That requires becoming emotionally self-aware.

Emotional self-awareness moves you from mastering your own emotions (and drivers), but also of the emotions of the people around you. It is what separates emotional win-win behavior and control from anger and denial.

One of the greatest gaps in our emotional behaviors is living in emotional denial. We often develop emotional defense mechanisms to safeguard our emotions or make it appear as if "nothing is wrong." Without emotional self-awareness, all our skills and competencies are just a way of at best entertaining ourselves, at worst deceiving ourselves. Emotional self-awareness paves the road for success.

As a young leader, when I was highly focused on developing my emotional intelligence, I would often reflect on my past emotional behaviors and examine what triggered the responses. I would also reflect on the emotional behaviors of others and their drivers. I felt the difficulty of the self and social-awareness challenge, but I was willing to pay the price to improve. Unfortunately, you do not build emotional intelligence overnight, but rather, it continues to be an ongoing process, a continuous self-development and self-management. I've matured under the weight of the journey. And my approach to addressing situations has changed so that my focus is not on my emotional triggers. It's on emotional self-management. It's on what I'm going to do to emotionally manage myself. To determine how emotionally intelligent you are, evaluate yourself based on the following statements as you actually are, rather than as you think.

	Not at all	Rarely	Sometimes	Often	Very Often
I can recognize my emotions as I experience them					
I lose my temper when I feel frustrated					
People have told me that I'm a good listener					
I know how to calm myself down when I feel anxious or upset					
I enjoy organizing groups					
I find it hard to focus on something over the long term					
I find it difficult to move on when I feel frustrated or unhappy					
I know my strengths and my weaknesses					
I avoid conflict and negotiations					
I feel that I don't enjoy my work					

I ask people for feedback on what I do well and how I can improve					
I set long-term goals and review my progress regularly					
I find it difficult to read other people's emotions					
I struggle to read other people's emotions					
I struggle to build rapport with others					
I use active listening skills when people speak to me.					

𝓕𝓞𝓤𝓡

Self-Management:

Managing Your Anger

*H*AVE YOU EVER SAT IN YOUR OFFICE as your manager just *lost* it, and either went on a tirade or got up and banged his head on the wall and used expletives? If you have had such an experience at work, you will understand the impact of that behavior and the rippling effect it has on the entire organization.

I remember working in an organization where the country manager, Joshua, would have frequent outbursts of anger in the office. Each time, he would leave his secretary and other employees traumatized. Many of the other employees would tip-toe around him to avoid uncomfortable incidents.

It is acceptable to have disagreements in the workplace and to show strong emotion. But it can be detrimental when people are overcome by their emotions and cannot control their behavior, resulting in harm to themselves and even to others.

What are some of the factors that can contribute to feeling angry in the workplace?

- The employee or manager is hot-tempered, and simple disappointments result in sudden outbursts
- The employee cannot live up to a supervisor's expectations because they are too high or continuously changing
- Employees are frequently criticized by their manager
- Employees are promised a salary increase or a promotion which is not fulfilled
- Employees are asked to do something that is outside their contractual agreements.

Dealing with anger

While there are various scenarios that can lead to anger, all employees are expected to act and communicate in an ethical and professional manner that is non-threatening to others in the workplace.

According to Donald Gibson of Fairfield University, who co-wrote *Managing Anger in the Workplace*, several strategies can be adopted for controlling anger.

- Avoid anger as much as possible. This does not mean suppressing your feelings, but rather improving your outlook on yourself and on life so that there are fewer situations in which you are likely to become angry

- Think about your anger and decide if it really makes sense, given the situation
- Control your physical response to anger by doing constructive things, such as exercising, getting enough sleep, and avoiding alcohol. The healthier you are, the more likely you are to respond appropriately to situations
- Let go of unmanageable anger. Many situations will be beyond your control, so it is important to let go of this type of anger. Ask yourself, "Can I resolve whatever it is that is causing this anger?" If you cannot, then you need to let it go.

If you feel anger and have a difficult time dealing with it, see if your company has an employee assistance program (EAP). EAP providers typically allow employees to see therapists in these circumstances.

Practice the following when anger strikes

- Take several deep breaths
- Repeat a calming word or phrase in your mind, such as "relax" or "stay calm"
- Slowly count to 10
- Ask yourself, "How would my favorite leader handle this situation?"

Increase your self-awareness and know your personal triggers

We are all guilty of having *hot buttons* that can trigger different emotions or responses without warning. The secret is gaining awareness of your personal triggers and recognizing them in time before they overwhelm you. If you can recognize them, you can learn when to walk away from situations that will make you angry, and you will make significant progress in controlling your anger.

Sometimes, you simply need to put some physical distance between yourself and the situation, to cool off. To do this, you WALK AWAY.

I remember having a heated discussion with an engineer. As he began to raise his voice, I realized my buttons were being pushed and I quickly decided to walk away from the situation.

After a trip to the mall, I was able to sit quietly, gather my thoughts, compose myself, and gain clarity. When I returned to the office, the engineer humbly apologized for his behavior.

Sometimes you need to walk away from a situation, to calm yourself and regain clarity.

Developing The Self-Esteem Person Within You

*J*ones worked as an administrative assistant in a medium-sized business. Throughout her stint with the company, she doubted her ability to formulate letters, interact with clients, or simply restructure her filing system. She was of the belief that everyone else was better than her.

These are common signs of a lack of confidence and low self-esteem on the job. The way Jones felt about herself directly affected her productivity and job performance, which in turn affected her career success.

According to the experts, people with a lack of confidence engage in subconscious behaviors that undermine their success. Lois Frankel, PhD, president of Corporate Coaching International and author of the bestselling book *Nice Girls Don't Get the Corner Office*, stated that people with low self-esteem often try to remain under the radar because they do not want to be noticed.

Having confidence, especially in the workplace, inspires creativity and courage. Low self-esteem means that you are less inclined to take risks when it comes to your career – and risk isn't always a bad thing. If you remain complacent, you will never advance or accomplish your career or personal goals.

Here are four signs and symptoms of low self-esteem according to the experts:

Insecurity and lack of belief in oneself

People who suffer from low self-esteem often feel insecure about themselves. They develop unreasonable expectations of those they work with, and often throw out tests and cues, expecting their colleagues to provide what they need.

Inability to trust others

One of the many symptoms of low self-esteem is the inability to trust others. Such people tend to feel that others are out to get them and are plotting against them.

Extreme inability to make decisions

People who lack confidence in themselves are always watchful and looking for cues as to how they imagine others want them to speak and act. They fear making a mistake and disappointing others who they feel are watching them.

Inadequacy leading to hypersensitivity

Another symptom of low self-esteem is hypersensitivity. Sufferers have a feeling that they are inadequate. They think that others feel the same way about them as they feel about themselves. They are quick to take offence when they read signs of people looking down upon them, mocking them, or taking advantage of them.

What strategies can be used to rebuild one's self-esteem, according to research

Become aware of your thoughts and beliefs

If you are not feeling the way you want to, STOP in that moment and ask yourself, "What am I thinking that is making me feel this way?" and "How is this way of thinking helping me?"

Consider another way you could think about what is happening that would make you feel better

How do you need to change the way you think to get what you want? You must start to master your thoughts if you want to master the results in your life; it is your mind-set that creates your reality.

Change limited thinking

Another technique is to catch yourself when you are thinking something limiting. Stop and tell yourself that this thought is not true, then rephrase the negative sentence in a positive way a few times. Then move forward.

There is a science behind this suggestion which is called neuro-plasticity: it is your brain's ability to start forming new neural connections which can have long-term effects on the way you habitually think.

Stop comparing yourself to others
This can lead to disillusionment and is nothing but a bad habit. There is only one of you, so be the best *you* that you can be. Start to show more support for yourself, as you would for a friend. Surround yourself with people who make you feel good: people who do not put you down or make you feel less worthy, but rather hold you up and cheer you on.

$\mathscr{SIX}$

A New Beginning:

Bouncing Back From A Job Loss

*G*ETTING LAID OFF IS PERHAPS the most traumatic professional experience a person can have. But it can also be the start of a new and exciting journey. Here's what the experts are saying.

According to John Lees, the UK-based career strategist and the author of *How to Get a Job You Love*, "Getting laid off is a manageable setback on the scale of human experience", and it can even lead to something positive. "Try to think about it as an opportunity that's ultimately going to do you some good," says Priscilla Claman, the president of Career Strategies, a Boston-based consulting firm and a contributor to the *HBR Guide to Getting the Right Job*. "A lot of people stay in their jobs for too long; they get stuck and can't move on." So a layoff can be seen as giving you a fresh start.

To help you bounce back from this difficult and often stressful situation, here is some research-based advice on the steps you should take immediately following a layoff.

Do nothing – at least for the first 48 hours

Today I was informed that I no longer have a job, and my first instinct is maybe to speak ill of my former employer on Facebook or Twitter, or to friends; or to immediately overhaul my LinkedIn profile and start applying for jobs.

STOP! These are not wise things to do. It is normal to feel hurt, angry, depressed, or anxious about what the future holds, but it is important to give yourself time to simply absorb what has occurred. Job loss and unemployment involve many changes all at once, which can rock your sense of purpose and self-esteem.

Think of your job loss as a temporary setback

Most successful people have experienced major setbacks in their careers, but have turned things around by picking themselves up, learning from the experience, and trying again. You can do the same.

Do a financial plan. Review your living expenses and eliminate all unnecessary items, including vacations, dining out, entertainment, new purchases such as furniture, etc. During unemployment, these are luxuries that you cannot afford until a new job is secured. Create a new *lean* lifestyle budget in writing, and stick to it.

Based on your adjusted lifestyle budget, determine how many months you can remain unemployed until your emergency reserves run out, taking into account any unemployment insurance benefits or severance payments that you are entitled to.

Talk it out

Talk with friends and family and let important people in your life know what is going on. Accepting help and support from people who care about you and will listen to you can help a lot. Keeping secrets is very stressful, and for most people having support and empathy is invaluable in navigating this emotional time.

Keep a positive mental attitude

Be aware of the messages that you are giving yourself. If you notice you are having self-critical thoughts (e.g. "I will never have a good job again", or "I feel worthless"), it is important to recognize this and to tell yourself to stop doing it. These thoughts are unhelpful and will only make you feel worse.

You cannot always be in control of what happens to you – in fact, how you handle what happens to you is often the only thing you *can* control. Remember that nothing ever stays the same, and tell yourself that this too shall pass.

Maintain a hopeful outlook and visualize what you want rather than worrying about what you fear.

Frame your layoff story

John Lees suggests that once you have moved past your initial layoff story, you should work on crafting a simple explanation for your layoff that you can share with professional contacts and potential hiring managers. Develop an "objective, short, and upbeat" message that shows you are "not a victim and you are not stuck".

Explore opportunities

Before you make any networking calls or answer job advertisements, you need to get yourself together. Reach out to former colleagues and friends who work for organizations that interest you. Try to get up-to-date on the latest issues and buzzwords from those people.

Also, think about all the head-hunters you know. Becoming a member of a professional association can be a good start. Network with an exploratory mind-set. Your goal is to find out what's going on in a given sector and organization, and learn what success looks like in it.

Tend to your wellbeing

The old cliché that looking for a job is a fulltime job holds some weight. Do not become obsessed with job hunting, since this can lead to unproductivity. Taking care of yourself is essential during this phase of your life. Ensure that you are eating well, and getting plenty of exercise. Remember to keep your spirits up and your energy high. Most importantly, be loving and kind to yourself. Do not beat yourself up and do not apportion blame to yourself. Speak about yourself with pride. Love yourself first!

$\mathcal{SEVEN}$

PROFESSIONAL GROWTH:

Becoming Teachable In The Workplace

*H*AVE YOU EVER WORKED with someone who does not take directions and thinks they are always right?

Consider this scenario. You have a co-worker who comes into work every day thinking she knows it all. She cannot figure out why she did not get that recent promotion. She strongly believes that management is satisfied with her performance and her work is *awesome*. You try to teach her something to improve her work, but it is useless. She assumes you are trying to sabotage her job and she chooses not to listen.

We all have co-workers like that, don't we?

What does it mean to be a "teachable employee"?

Teachable employees have a teachable spirit. According to John C Maxwell, "You must have a teachable spirit. If you don't, you will come to the end of your potential long before you come to the end of your life."

Teachable employees use every situation (good or bad) and every criticism as an opportunity to learn and grow. They turn negative experiences into positive life lessons which help build their knowledge base and add value to the lives of others.

How can I become teachable?

An employee can become teachable by cultivating the following traits.

Teachable people have an attitude conducive to learning

The attitude you carry into your office sets the tone and direction for everything you do.

A former co-worker, Elizabeth, often walked around with a negative can't-do-it attitude in the office. If you asked her to send an email, she believed she was not competent enough. Her approach to each task, from ordering stationery supplies to maintaining a proper filing system, often resulted in complete failure because of her attitude.

Your attitudes are the way you approach situations, and the way you approach situations will determine your success or failure. So if you keep your mind open to new things, and let your attitude be expectant, you will begin to use each opportunity to learn something new.

As Elizabeth continued to perform her daily duties, she remained closed-minded and missed great opportunities. Remember, a negative attitude rarely creates positive change.

Teachable people have a beginner's mindset

What do all beginners have in common? They know they don't know it all, and that shapes the way they approach situations. As a result, they are open, humble, and lacking in the rigidity that often accompanies achievement.

Chris had 20 years' experience as a training instructor for an organization. His teaching method did not include the use of PowerPoint presentations. The company decided to improve their training delivery style and suggested that Chris convert his handwritten notes into a PowerPoint presentation. Chris became very upset and said, "I have been doing this for over 20 years, you can't tell me how to do my work."

This was a wrong mindset, especially since every day the world keeps on evolving and there will always be something new to learn.

When you adopt a beginner-mindset approach, you become more open and enjoy learning new things along the way. To assist you in maintaining this beginner's mindset, try to keep the following three things in mind:

- Everyone has something to teach me
- Every day I have something to learn
- Every time I learn something, I benefit.

Teachable people take long, hard looks in the mirror

A new instructor joined the team and was about to deliver his first training session. Anxious to kick-start the training, he began taking short-cuts without informing colleagues. This created chaos.

Before pointing fingers, I remember sitting in the office and asking myself, "Where did I go wrong, am I the cause?" This approach helped me to evaluate all procedures followed, in order to determine where the problem began.

When was the last time you honestly and openly evaluated yourself? Becoming and remaining teachable requires you to honestly and openly evaluate yourself on a continual basis.

Any time you face a challenge, loss, or problem, one of the first things you need to ask yourself is, "Am I the cause?" This is a key component to teachability. If the answer is yes, then you need to be ready to make changes. When people refuse to look in the mirror, and instead look to other people or situations to blame, they keep getting the same results over and over.

Teachable people encourage others to speak into their lives

Nobody likes it when people speak truth that might be hurtful into their lives, and when someone has the courage to speak up, we attack them.

We need to react differently. Teachable people need to surround themselves with people who know them well and who will lovingly, yet honestly, speak into their lives. That can be a challenge, for many reasons. Columnist Doug Larson said, "Wisdom is the reward you get for a lifetime of listening when you would have preferred to talk."

Teachable people learn something new every day

The secret to any person's success can be found in his or her daily agenda. Do you have a daily agenda? Do you plan your day, or do you go with the flow?

People grow and improve, not by huge leaps and bounds, but by small, incremental changes. Children's advocate Marian Wright Edelman said, "We must not, in trying to think about how we can make a big difference, ignore the small daily differences we can make which, over time, add up to big differences that we often cannot foresee."

Teachable people try to leverage this truth by learning something new every day. A single day is enough to make us a little larger or a little smaller. The habits you practice every day will make you or break you. If you want to become a teachable person who learns from losses, then make learning your daily habit. It may not change your life in a day. But it will change your days for life.

ℰℐ𝒢ℋ𝒯

A Guide to Overcoming Leadership Challenges

ONE DAY I WAS SITTING IN A BOARDROOM with 20 leaders from different organizations. I could tell they were very successful; each person took pride in describing their roles and responsibilities. Dr Bill walked into the room and said, "So what, you are a leader, what does it mean

? What does leadership mean?" There was complete silence in the room for two minutes. Joanne responded, "I have a leadership position in my organization, I am the quality manager, nothing can be approved without my signature." I agreed that quality was critical to the success of any organization. But a job position and leadership should not be confused.

Leadership has nothing to do with one's position in the hierarchy of an organization or with one's seniority. A job title or someone's personal attributes do not automatically qualify him to be a leader; and leadership is not management.

Peter Drucker asserts that "A leader is someone who has followers." I disagree. I have had the opportunity to work in a military environment, where routine orders were given by the commander to his subordinates, and the troops were mandated to follow those orders. I strongly oppose the view that this made the commander a leader.

Warren Bennis opines that "Leadership is the capacity to translate vision into reality." However, for a carnival/events organizer, every Carnival season produces a vision for a large parade of bands, with lots of promotional events both local and international. It becomes a reality. Are you a leader? No, you're a carnival/events organizer.

According to John C Maxwell, "Being a great leader is all about having a genuine willingness and a true commitment to lead others to achieve a common vision and goals through positive influence. No leader can ever achieve anything great or long-lasting all alone. Teamwork goes hand in hand with leadership. Leadership is *about* people – and *for* people."

When there is a lack of leadership, there is a lack of influence, and many challenges arise. Here are some examples.

Developing the relevant skills to manage effectively can be a challenge

Many years ago, Jane, a colleague of mine, was promoted to marketing manager. She was very passionate about her job, and her excellent work ethic got her the position. But Jane began to struggle with time management, prioritization, strategic thinking, and decision-making; as a result, she was unable to get up to speed with the job.

Inability to motivate others and get employees to work smarter

One of my students once said to me, "Working at the bank is such a challenge, there is no motivation, there is no desire to get to work on time, so employees arrive late, leave early, and the bank suffers with a high employee turnover."

Inability to guide change

Some leaders have the challenge of managing, mobilizing, understanding and leading change. Guiding change includes knowing how to mitigate consequences, overcome resistance to change, and deal with employees' reactions to change.

Managing internal stakeholders and politics

Some leaders find it difficult to manage relationships, politics, and image. This challenge includes gaining managerial support and getting buy-in from other departments, groups or individuals.

Levels of leadership

Overcoming the above challenges requires an in-depth understanding of the different levels of leadership. According to John C Maxwell, there are five.

Level 1: position

This is the lowest level of leadership – the entry level. People who make it only to Level 1 may be bosses, but they are never leaders. They have subordinates, not team members. They rely on rules, regulations, policies, and organizational charts to control their people. Their people will only follow them within the stated boundaries of their authority.

Position is the only level that does not require ability and effort to achieve. Anyone can be appointed to a position. This means that position is a fine starting point, but every leader should aspire to grow beyond Level 1.

Level 2: permission

Making the shift from *position* to *permission* is a person's first real step into leadership. Leadership is influence, and when a leader learns to function on the permission level, everything changes. People do more than merely comply with orders. They actually start to follow their leader. And they do so because they really want to. Why? Because the leader begins to influence people with relationship, not just position.

When people feel liked, cared for, included, valued, and trusted, they begin to work together with their leader and each other. And that can change the entire working environment. The old saying is really true: people go along with leaders they get along with.

Level 3: production

Production separates true leaders from people who merely occupy leadership positions. Good leaders always make things happen. They get results. They can make a significant impact on an organization. Not only are they productive individually, but they can also help the team produce. No one can fake Level 3. Either you're producing for the organization and adding to its bottom line (whatever that may be), or you're not.

Some people never move up from Level 2 *permission* to Level 3 *production*. Why? They can't seem to produce results. When that is the case, it's usually because they lack the self-discipline, work ethic, organization, or skills to be productive. However, if you want to go to higher levels of leadership, you simply have to produce. There is no way around it.

Level 4: people development

At Level 3, the emphasis is on personal and corporate productivity. The ability to create a high-productivity team, department, or organization indicates a higher level of leadership ability than most others display. But to reach the upper levels of leadership that create elite organizations, leaders must transition from being *producers* to being *developers*. Why? Because people are any organization's most appreciable asset.

Good leaders at Level 4 invest their time, energy, money, and thinking into growing others as leaders. How does this emphasis on people and people-decisions translate into action? Leaders on the people development level of leadership shift their focus from the production achieved by others to the development of their potential. They put only 20 per cent of their focus on their personal productivity, and the other 80 per cent on developing and leading others.

This can be a difficult shift for highly productive people who are used to getting their hands dirty. But it's a change that can revolutionize an organization and give it a much brighter future.

Level 5: the pinnacle

Rare is the leader who reaches Level 5, the *pinnacle*. Not only is leadership at this level a culmination of leading well on the other four levels, but it also requires both a high degree of skill and some amount of natural leadership ability.

It takes a lot to be able to develop other leaders so that they reach Level 4; that's what Level 5 leaders do. The individuals who reach Level 5 lead so well for so long that they create a legacy of leadership in the organization they serve.

Pinnacle leaders stand out from everyone else. They are a cut above, and they seem to bring success with them wherever they go. Leadership at this high level lifts the entire organization and creates an environment that benefits everyone in it, contributing to their success. Level 5 leaders often possess an influence that transcends the organization and the industry the leader works in.

Most leaders who reach the pinnacle do so late in their careers. But this level is not a resting place for leaders to stop and view their success. It is a reproducing place from which they make the greatest impact of their lives. That's why leaders who reach the pinnacle should make the most of it while they can. With gratitude and humility, they should lift up as many leaders as they can, tackle as many great challenges as possible, and extend their influence to make a positive difference beyond their own organization and industry.

Nine

Tips For Working With A Toxic Boss

OES YOUR CAREER ADVANTAGES worth the pain of working with a toxic supervisor?

Here's what the experts say, according the *Harvard Business Review.* "There's a difference between a difficult employee and a toxic one," states Dylan Minor, an assistant professor at the Kellogg School of Management, who studies this topic. "I call them toxic because not only do they cause harm but they also spread their behavior to others." Christine Porath adds: "There's a pattern of de-energizing, frustrating or putting down teammates."

Toxic bosses can cause irrevocable damage to their companies and employees, and can have a significant impact on performance. Some enjoy smugly manipulating employees and using them as instruments to advance their own interests.

Successful people, however, do not allow toxic bosses to deter them, because they understand that to win the game you must simply know how to play the hand you have been dealt. When that hand is a toxic boss, successful people identify the type of toxic boss they are working for and then use this information to neutralize their boss's behavior.

Here are some strategies that successful people use to work effectively with various types of toxic boss.

The inappropriate buddy

Jason is your boss, and he is overly friendly – and not in the fun, team-building sort of way. He is constantly inviting you to hang out with him outside work, and engages in unnecessary office gossip. He uses his influence to make friends at the expense of his work. He chooses favorites and creates divisions among employees, who become frustrated by the imbalance in attention and respect.

How to neutralize an inappropriate buddy

The most important thing to do with this type of boss is to set firm boundaries. Do not allow yourself to be intimidated by his job title. By consciously and proactively establishing a boundary, you can take control of the situation. You can remain friendly with your boss all day, for example, without being afraid to say no to drinks after work. By distancing yourself from behavior that you deem inappropriate, you can still succeed and even have a healthy relationship with your boss.

Balance is important in these situations. It is important not to put up unnecessary boundaries that stop you from being seen as friendly (ideally, as a friend).

The micromanager

Your boss Ashley makes you feel as if you are under constant surveillance. This micromanager pays too much attention to small details, and her constant hovering makes employees feel discouraged, frustrated, and even uncomfortable.

How to neutralize a micromanager

Successful people appeal to micromanagers by proving themselves to be flexible, competent, and disciplined, while staying in constant communication. A micromanager is naturally drawn to the employee who produces work the way she imagines it. The challenge with the micromanager is grasping just what she is imagining. To do this, try asking specific questions about your project, check in frequently, and look for trends in the micromanager's feedback.

The Tyrant

Candace, the tyrant boss, resorts to Machiavellian tactics and constantly makes decisions that feed her ego. Her primary concern is maintaining power, and she will coerce and intimidate others to do so. Candace classifies people in her mind and treats them accordingly. High achievers who challenge her thinking are treated as mutinous, while those who support her achievements with gestures of loyalty find themselves in the position of first mate.

How to neutralize a tyrant

A painful but effective strategy with the tyrant is to present your ideas in a way that lets her to take partial credit. The tyrant can then maintain her ego without having to shut down your idea. Also, to survive a tyrant, you must choose your battles wisely. If you practice self-awareness and manage your emotions, you can rationally choose which battles are worth fighting and which ones you should just let go of.

The Incompetent

Steve is a boss who promotes hastily or hires haphazardly, and holds a position that is beyond his capabilities. He may not be completely incompetent, but he has people reporting to him who have been at the company a lot longer and have information and skills that he lacks.

How to neutralize an incompetent

If you find yourself frustrated with this type of boss, it is probably because you have experience that he lacks. It is important to swallow your pride and share your experience and knowledge, without rubbing it in his face. Share the information that this boss needs in order to grow into his role, and you will become his ally and confidant.

The Seagull

The seagull manager is one who swoops in and squawks up a storm. He does not take time to get the facts straight and work alongside the team to realize a viable solution. The seagull deposits steaming piles of formulaic advice and then abruptly takes off, leaving everyone else behind to clean up the mess. Seagulls interact with their employees only when there's a fire to put out.

How to neutralize a seagull

A good strategy would be getting the team to discuss with him the implications of his abrupt approach to solving problems. If the entire group bands together and provides constructive, non-threatening feedback, the seagull will more often than not find a better way to work with his team. It's easy to spot a seagull when you're on the receiving end of his airborne dumps, but the manager doing the squawking is often unaware of the negative impact of his behavior. Have the group give him a little nudge, and things are bound to change for the better.

TEN

Are You Where You Want To Be In Life?

FOR EVERY CLIENT, SUCCESS IS DEFINED differently, so the coaching process will be different for each person. It could involve changing careers, making your dreams become a reality, negotiating different responsibilities in a current role, building your level of influence, or making a larger-scale life change toward a new way of living. Whichever way, you need to ask the right questions and have the right strategies to move forward.

What do you want and how are you going to get there?

Do you know what you want in the next year, five years, or ten years in your career? If you don't have a career development plan in place, create one. Include upward moves, lateral moves, and any additional skills, education or certification you want to acquire. Having an idea of your future destination increases the chances of actually getting there.

What are you good at, what are your skills and your strengths?

What skills do you use in your current role? What other skills do you have? Which of these are transferable to other roles or industries? How would you summarize what strengths you bring to leadership, managing others, or working with a team? Ask colleagues and friends for feedback. Then take a course, read a book, or hire a coach to help you to start to improve your skills and add new ones.

Know your work values

Values define what is most important to you. They are the basis on which you make decisions and form the motivations behind your work. When your values are not aligned with the values of your organization/team, you feel frustrated. There may be cultural differences, differences in environmental philosophies, or work ethic issues. Whatever the case, aligning your core work values with your career is vitally important to long-term job success. What values are most important to you, and how can you prioritize those in your career?

Cultivate your leadership style

A leadership style is less about your needs, and more about how well you succeed in your organization. Whether you are an experienced leader or just starting out in your career, having a recognizable leadership style will allow you to achieve maximum effectiveness at work. Get to know different leadership styles, and when they are used most effectively. Understand which style feels the most authentic to you, and actively work to stretch yourself into the styles you find harder.

Develop your professional brand image

Your professional brand is the outward image and style of who you are. It is reflected in how you communicate, act, and dress. It conveys a powerful message to those around you. If your professional brand is not on par with your colleagues, or does not match the career you are moving into, take steps to change it. That could involve a more professional style if you are moving upwards into a corporate career, or a more casual style if you are moving to a non-profit organization, or into education, for instance.

Cultivate your professional network

Your professional network is the community that can give you access to information, contacts, and jobs. The key is to develop the network *before* you need it. Actively build a network of peers in your current field, and in any field you are considering for a lateral move. LinkedIn is a great tool for making online connections. In addition, find professional associations and networking groups that align with your career interests.

Find a mentor

A mentor is a person with more experience in business, or simply in life, who can advise you on career development and navigating new work challenges. Seek out a mentor who is a good fit with your career goals – someone who is at least five to ten years ahead of you. A mentor who aligns with your work values and has had a similar career path would be ideal.

Take action

The big picture of where your career is headed can be difficult to see clearly. The key to navigating any long-term goal is to break it down into small action steps with short timeframes. Think of one thing you can do this week to move your career-thinking forward a notch. Take an assessment, seek out new professional connections, or enroll in a course. Taking action will get you successfully creating your ideal career path.

ELEVEN

Charting Your Career Path

*J*ONES WORKED WITHIN THE MEDICAL INDUSTRY and had lost interest in her job. She admitted that a career change was needed urgently, but was unsure about the best approach to use. Some of her questions centered on the industry or field she should venture into: when would it be safe to make the shift? Should she really go, or should she give her current job another try?

We often assume that the key to a successful career change is knowing what we want and allowing our knowledge to guide our actions. In fact, change often occurs the other way round. Doing comes first, knowing second. The following steps can guide you through the process of charting your career.

Plan and implement change strategy

Firstly, you need to determine with clarity and certainty what you want to do. Secondly, use that knowledge to identify jobs or fields in which your passions can be coupled with your skills and experience. Seeking advice from professionals requires us to clear significant hurdles such as a deeply ingrained tendency to prefer our own opinions, irrespective of our talent, and the fact that careful listening is hard and time-consuming work. Those who are truly open to guidance develop solutions to problems much better and faster than they would have done on their own.

Know yourself

Knowing, in theory, comes from self-reflection and solitary introspection. Learning whether we are introverted or extroverted, whether we prefer to work in a structured and methodical environment or in chaos, whether we place greater value on impact or income, will help us avoid jobs that will prove unsatisfying. Reviewing our past careers and identifying our likes and dislikes can be a very useful tool.

Let go of the thinking, patterns and behaviors that keep you stuck

At times, you may let your thinking patterns and behaviors keep you in bondage. You need to dig deep within to determine what is holding you back from becoming more successful in your career.

One of the first things to do is identify any negative patterns in your life, such as a toxic work environment, being continually passed over, or draining responsibilities. Observe the patterns and try to see how you are helping to sustain them; then do something concrete to change that dynamic. Be accountable and take action to generate change.

You may have limited ideas about your success and your worth, or you may be repeating actions that hold you back from the next level of success. For many people, the problem is with their boundaries – an inability to advocate for and honor their priorities. For others, their communication style may be hurting them, pushing away any kind of positive support or help. For others still, it's a lack of confidence, or a belief that they are *less than* and not worthy of advancing or experiencing joy and satisfaction in their work.

Until you let go of whatever you are doing and thinking that keeps you stuck and small, you cannot build a happy, successful career. Your limitations will follow you in every new direction until you address them.

Consult trusted advisers

If you accept the conventional wisdom that career change begins with self-knowledge and proceeds through an objective scrutiny of the available choices, who should you turn to for guidance?

Friends and family can often add a dose of pragmatism and keep you grounded in the realities of the marketplace. To make a true break with the past, we need to reassess ourselves. We need guides who have been there and have an appreciation of where we are going. Looking outside our normal circles to new people, networks, and professional communities is key to changing the status quo and getting psychological sustenance.

Is big better?

We often assume that we can leap directly from a desire for change to a single decision that will reinvent us. Conventional wisdom might say you should not fool yourself with small, superficial adjustments. But trying to tackle the big changes too quickly can be counterproductive. Just as starting the transition by looking for one's true self can cause paralysis rather than progress, trying to make one big move, once and for all, can prevent real change.

It takes time to discover what we truly want to change, and to identify the deeply grooved habits and assumptions that are holding us back.

Shifting connections

Consider how common it is for employees to say of their companies, "There is no one here I want to be like." Shifting connections refers to the practice of finding people who can help us see and grow into our new selves. For most of the successful career changers I have observed, there has been a guiding figure or new professional community to help to light the way and cushion the eventual leap.

Making sense

In the middle of the confusion about which way to go, many of us hope for one event that will clarify everything, that will transform our stumbling moves into a coherent trajectory. But we can create our own triggers for change, by infusing events – the momentous and the mundane – with special meaning and weaving them into a story about who we are becoming. Trigger events don't just jolt us out of our habitual routines: they are the necessary pegs on which to hang our reinvention stories.

Create it SMART

Finally, going from point A to point Z takes time. The process involves identifying who you really are and determining the directions that will align best with your values, visions and needs. This requires time, energy, patience, trust and commitment. You've got to be ready to turn yourself inside out and stretch and expand yourself if you want great success in your work.

You also need a 3-month, 6-month and 12-month plan, with specific, measurable, achievable, realistic, and timely goals (SMART goals), and someone in your court to hold you accountable. Get help, build a plan with milestones that you can measure, and get on the path to expanding yourself so that you are a true match with the great career you long for.

Is successful career change possible for you? Yes – but only if you're ready to do the work. Those who fantasies about doing meaningful, lucrative work they love, but who will not commit themselves to the process and the journey of change, will never get out of the starting gate.

TWELVE

Your Road Map To Success

WHAT DOES SUCCESS LOOK LIKE to you? Are you taking the right steps to achieve success in your life?

These are two important questions we must ask ourselves as we work towards achieving success. Quite often, we would like to be successful but choose instead to spend our day focusing on activities or people that do not contribute to our success.

Here are a few tips to consider as you move closer to achieving success.

Tip 1: Carefully examine your daily activities

What activities can you eliminate from your life because they do not support your goals? Let's be honest: many times we spend time surfing the internet, playing games, sleeping, hanging out with friends, performing monotonous tasks, dreaming, wishing for the life we have always wanted ... and the list goes on.

In order to achieve success, you must first focus on the important goals in your life. Are they SMART goals? How does your daily activity bring you closer to achieving these goals? If your answer to those two questions is no, then develop SMART goals and eliminate the time-wasting activities.

You must align all your activities to the achievement of your goals and have a clear focus on what you want to achieve. This will require you to eliminate the things or people that are holding you back. Always push yourself beyond the limits.

Tip 2: Do what successful people do

If you want to be like people who are successful in life, do what successful people do; do not settle for the average. "Average" is one of the most notorious and often undetected robbers of dreams, visions, goals and ideas. Let us consider some of the activities of successful people that you can adopt:

- Read about your industry and beyond
- Work out for a strong body, which supports a strong mind
- Remove fear
- Unplug without a device
- Check your pride at the door
- Never give up
- Surround yourself with positive people
- Listen and learn
- Put in extra effort to stay organized
- Pay attention to details

- Keep some balance in your life
- Write down your gratitude
- Deprioritize opportunities which do not fit with your goals
- Adapt to what the present holds
- Pick three things to do each day.

Tip 3: Identify successful people who are living your dream, and align yourself with them

Success leaves tracks, and you can follow them step by step to achieve your very own success.

A Step Closer To Achieving Success

"People do not become successful by chance. They pound the pavements day and night, build resilience, chase after skills, and prepare for opportunities." –
Sally Ann Bharat

SOME OF THE BIGGEST and most common obstacles to achieving the success you want, or improving your life, are the limiting beliefs that hold you back; not taking action; and being too hard on yourself.

"Limiting beliefs" may not be the sexiest or most exciting expression, but it constitutes the belief system that impoverishes your life. It is that running dialogue in your head that says:

- I lack motivation
- I am not good enough to be successful or to do anything special
- I am too old to change
- It is too late to go back and study
- I have no clue where to start
- I am too dumb to get anywhere
- Everyone else is better than I am.

Take responsibility for your beliefs and start shifting those negative thoughts into new and positive ones.

Think and speak positively

Each morning when I wake up, I begin with positive affirmations that brighten my day. I feel empowered, and believe and know that I can do anything I set my mind to do.

When I begin on a positive note, I attract positive energy. Tasks that seemed so difficult are now less of a challenge. I can overcome obstacles and identify lessons that can be learnt in the process.

These results come from that positive energy, from believing in myself and taking consistent action. I feel a lot less pressure on myself. I am more relaxed and prone to continue, which is not the case if I fixate on potential results that never come as quickly as I want, and if I am afraid to launch out into choppy waters.

Remind yourself that you must take action

Find your top priorities and the reasons that inspire you to do what you are doing. In order to stay focused and not lose track of why you are taking action:

- *Write down your most important reasons.* Take a few minutes, sit down with paper and a pen, and write down the top one to three reasons why you take action and want to keep doing what you are doing in your life right now.

- *Put that note where you can see it every day.* Put it somewhere like your workspace, or near your bed, so that you see it every morning when you wake up.

- *Take smaller steps on the days when the big ones seem too daunting.* On some days, getting started with any of the most important tasks may seem daunting. So you begin to procrastinate. When that happens, one thing that has worked for me is to be kind to myself. I gently nudge myself forward instead of beating myself up. At times like these I take:

- *A small step.* I may make a deal with myself to just work for five minutes on part of a bigger and more difficult task. Or:

- *An even smaller step.* If even that small step feels like too much and I start to procrastinate, I make a deal with myself to do one or two minutes of work. Sometimes that results in a few dents being made in a big task, or a couple of smaller tasks being completed; many breaks are taken during the day. The key is to keep moving forwards instead of standing still.

Celebrate what you did today

When you appreciate your good work, you feel even better about your life and yourself.

And over time, taking more action with less inner resistance becomes possible, and you associate action with more positive emotions than you did before.

Take two minutes at the end of the day to appreciate what you did today. Or write down a couple of self-appreciative things in your journal. Reward yourself for the things you did right today, to strengthen your habit of taking action. And remember to be kind to yourself for the things you may have missed or which did not get done. There is no point in trying to punish yourself, and even less benefit in trying to be perfect.

Try to see what you can learn from setbacks. Try another solution tomorrow and see if that yields better results.

THIRTEEN

DO IT NOW ATTITUDE

WHEN I WAS GROWING UP, my father always encouraged me to have a do-it-now attitude. Procrastination was never an option. "Later", I was told, is a dream-killer.

This approach created a sense of urgency in every task I undertook, and helped me to develop the power of positive thinking. It also allowed me to overcome my fears in order to achieve success.

Self-awareness

To grow yourself, you must first know yourself. When you have a good grasp of your strengths, weaknesses, blind spots and biases, you are better equipped to improve yourself, to add value to those around you and by extension your organization.

By contrast, lack of self-awareness can lead to confusion, and can also be very toxic to both you and those around you. Having greater self-awareness allowed me to zone in on key areas that needed improvement, to overcome limiting beliefs and look at things from different perspectives.

Self-discipline

John C Maxwell asserts that "We are responsible for ruling our actions and decisions. To make consistently good decisions, to take the right action when needed and to refrain from the wrong actions, requires character and self-discipline."

All great success in life, according to Brian Tracey, is preceded by long, sustained periods of focused effort on a single goal, the most important goal, with the determination to stay with the process until it is complete.

Adopting this approach at an early stage in life took me from an associate's degree to a doctorate, from the corporate world to my own company. The key thing was remaining focused on the most important task in front of me. I soon realized that there was no goal I could not accomplish and no task I could not complete.

Becoming comfortably uncomfortable

Neale Donald Walsh wisely said, "Life begins at the end of your comfort zone."

However, some folks prefer to remain in an environment where they are in control of their situation, have a steady level of performance, and experience low levels of anxiety and stress.

But then, how can you unleash your full potential? The day I lost my job is the day I began to live. I acquired greater skills, knowledge and opportunities than ever before. Life became lively, and I was able to break away from mental boundaries in order to make my dreams become a reality.

The Choices We Make, Make Us

Classmates and co-workers: "So, where do you live?"
Me: "I live in Laventille ..."
Classmates and co-workers (gasping): "What's that like!?"

OST OF THE TIME, people are astounded when they learn where I was born and raised. Okay, "astound" may not be the best word, but they are definitely surprised. I mean, how in the world do you live within a depressed community that has a high crime rate and a bad reputation, and continue to make the best choices that take you away from a life of crime and criminal activities?

If I'm being completely honest, I don't have an answer for you (*God* would be my best answer). But what I would say is that there is something we all have from the day we are born: choice! The choices you make, make you!

I have sat in the same room with people from depressed communities. I've also sat with bankers, professors, doctors, lawyers, consultants, CEOs, pilots, etc. Of course, you get your typical person who has not yet decided what the next step in their career is going to be. Nonetheless, one thing remains the same: we all have choices.

We all made a choice that made us who we are. Many of us made choices that have had lasting value; for others, their choices prevented them from achieving their goals. As for me, I have chosen to learn from the good choices those around me have made, as well as from their poor choices.

No, you didn't read that wrong ... *I learn from these people. Men and women alike. Their words have value. Their stories have weight. There are lessons to be learned.*

Over the years, these stories have added so much value to my life that they motivated me to positively impact the lives of others. Looking back, I can now say that my choices and decisions allowed me to set high standards for myself, much higher than others would set for me.

Of course, we all go through that process of having limiting beliefs; we sometimes think that we are not good enough or will never be good enough. The question of whether or not I should continue pursuing my dreams often swirled around in my head when I met a stumbling block ... *the choices we make, make us. You have got to believe in who you are.*

Sometimes, I agree, we make bad choices. We often brim with misery and regret when we realize our mistake. That's part of being human. When I reminisce about the past and review the things I once engaged in, instead of being ashamed of who I was or what I have done, I look back and realize that I have grown, and I wear my failures as a badge to remind me of who I am, where I came from, and what I have become today.

No one can undo the past, but we can always learn from it. Hindsight, after all, is 20/20 vision. Choices are the building blocks of our lives, and despite all the mistakes we make, each new day brings with it new opportunities and a whole new world of choices.

The choice to grow: deciding to grow every day by developing your strengths

We can choose whether to focus on our personal growth. If I am being honest, most young men and women today take investment in their personal growth and development for granted. They allow sabotaging self-doubt and negative influences to blur their decision-making, and simply settle for mediocrity.

But we as a people have the privilege of making that choice, choosing to invest in our growth and development in order to get the greatest return, focusing on our efforts to grow in those areas where our natural ability intersects with our natural affinity.

The choice of partnership: deciding to add value *to* others before expecting value *from* others

Quite often, we do things for others with an expectation of being rewarded in some way. Because of this expectation, we prevent ourselves from adding value to others for fear of getting nothing in return.

But when you make a habit of helping others to reach their goals, they will eventually help you attain your own. Far too often, I have seen leaders within organizations more concerned with climbing the ladder to success than connecting with others. Rather than trying to climb quickly to the top, they would be better served focusing attention on how to help others achieve success. On life's journey, you will always go faster alone, but you will inevitably go farther in partnership with others.

Remember that the choice is yours.

It has always been.

FIFTEEN

What Is Your Defining Moment?

SOME YEARS AGO, I DECIDED to pursue a doctorate at the University of The West Indies. I was filled with fear, mainly because I lacked both confidence in myself and the requisite managerial experience. I was intensely aware that this decision would have an enormous impact on my future and would be pivotal in the direction my life would take. I also knew that if I could do this, I would show my relatives and my future children that anything is possible.

Four years later, a friend screamed at me in anger, "You are always giving advice, motivating people, it's overwhelming for me." Those words seared my soul; their effect was beyond measure.

Three days later, I discovered my passion and signed up to become an independent coach, speaker, and trainer with the John C Maxwell Group.

In hindsight, these two events in my life turned me into a leader who can bounce back quickly from tough situations while maintaining laser-like focus. I am thankful that I was able to understand and recognize that they were defining moments, and that I knew how to harness them to propel me forward.

What is a defining moment?

According to *Forbes Magazine,* a defining moment is a point in your life when you are urged to make a pivotal decision, or when you experience something that fundamentally changes you. Not only do these moments define us, but they have a transformative effect on our perceptions and behaviors.

Moments that are truly defining will force you to ask "Why?" They will often challenge your beliefs/norms, and force you to behave differently.

How do leaders move forward?

Think of a moment when your true character was revealed, when you had an opportunity to excel, or you saw something with greater clarity. Inevitably, the road of life will be bumpy, testing your commitment to your purpose. But some individuals see bumps in the road as obstacles, while others see them as opportunities.

Leaders quickly recognize their defining moments and move forward by:

• *Being resilient and embracing adversity.* The irony of a defining moment is that if you don't define it, it will surely define you. View these moments as opportunities to learn and grow, and do not let them cause you to stagnate.

Compartmentalize the moment and quickly find purpose in it. For example, my friend's comments made me a highly committed personal growth and development advocate.

• *Acknowledging fear.* Best-selling author and entrepreneur Tim Ferriss says, "What we fear doing most is usually what we most need to do." The beauty of a defining moment is that it usually forces us to face our fears head-on and take action. I can personally attest to how scary it is, but also how much better you will become. Acknowledging fear helps mitigate the potential paralyzing effects.

• *Quickly recalibrating.* Recalibrating is a function of taking an honest assessment of where you are. To move forward, we often need to know why something occurred. But sometimes, we are unable to identify our *why* as quickly as we would like. With stillness and meditation come clarity and answers. Your *why* is the foundation for building your action plan to move forward. It is essential to think beyond the defining moment and open yourself up to the innumerable lessons.

• *Creating a solutions-based action plan.* Billionaire magnate, investor, engineer, and inventor Elon Musk is known for creating action plans. From a business perspective, action plans are essential to help us benchmark progress.

In 2004, prior to entering graduate school, I did a personal SWOT analysis to assess my skill sets and gaps. By doing this, I was able to identify my personal strengths and weaknesses, while at the same time assessing what could be viewed as either an opportunity or a threat to me. I was thus able to begin my studies with the end in mind, fully aware of what was required of me to complete my studies successfully.

Your plan does not have to be complex, but it must be specific. It's your roadmap for moving forward, and it lets you know how far you have come. Each year since 2004 I have continued to do a SWOT analysis to monitor my personal progress.

So long as we identify them quickly, and make the decision to move forwards, we all have the ability to define our defining moments.

SIXTEEN

Change Your World
And The World Around You Will
Change

> *"I don't think of myself as being poor and having a lucky break. I think of myself as someone who, from an early age, knew I had to be intentional about my personal growth, and invest heavily in ME. The best investment ever made was in ME"* –
> *Sally Ann Bharat*

E ARE OFTEN LASER FOCUSED on changing the world. But when we change our own world, the world around us will change.

How is this done?

The short version is simply this: you have to be a passionate eater, be ready to throttle your predators, and be absolutely beautiful – that's a given. The long version is that I actually have only five rules. You don't need to have money to be a passionate eater, you don't need to be a champion in all that you do; but if you want to excel in anything that you do, then these rules are for you.

My first rule is: find your passion

Do not worry about what the world needs. Rather ask yourself, "What drives me, what compels my emotion?" If you don't know what drives you, you will drift around and feel very unhappy.

I grew up in Laventille, Trinidad, a depressed community known for gang wars. Reprisal killings occurred on a regular basis. The stigma attached to Laventille made it very difficult to secure proper jobs; nationally, economic conditions resulted in thousands of people losing their work.

Despite these circumstances, I wanted to be different. But how do you do that?

One day, I was looking at television and saw Oprah Winfrey. She made a profound statement that had me mesmerized. *"The Big Secret in Life is that there is NO BIG SECRET IN LIFE. Whatever your goal, you can get there if you are willing to work."*

I wanted to become like Oprah Winfrey. I wanted to help others globally, I wanted to have my own television programme where I could listen to other people's career challenges, their life stories, and add value in the best possible way I could.

But I come from a poor family of ten siblings. My father died when I was five. I had no money, no one in the family chased after an education, and I did not have the entry qualifications for the University of the West Indies.

One day, I was fortunate enough to land a job at a helicopter company. I immediately enrolled in college to pursue an associate's degree. I worked an 8-to-4 job and studied for eight hours a day with two or three hours sleep for 14 years.

Eventually, I got all my degrees, from associates to master's, and I am in the process of completing a doctorate in business administration. I also gained an additional qualification: I became an executive director with The John Maxwell Team, which allowed me to be internationally certified and recognized as a trainer, keynote speaker and coach.

I had found my passion: to help others believe in themselves. Not only did I want to motivate people – I also wanted to transform lives globally and become internationally known. I did whatever it took to make my dreams become a reality.

In 2014, I was diagnosed with a skin disorder that was accompanied by excruciating pain. But I believed *no pain no gain,* and so I studied despite the pain. I was willing to work long and hard to achieve my dreams.

Discover your passion, and everything will fall into place. When obstacles present themselves, that burning desire will help you to be resilient and to continue chasing your dreams.

My second rule: never ever underestimate what you can do or who you can become

You have to believe in who you are and what you can do. You have to shoot for the stars. I never underestimated what I could do or who I could become. I wanted to do what Oprah Winfrey did. I wanted to be like John C Maxwell, I wanted to create transformation in the lives of others globally, I wanted to be coached and mentored by the best in the world. What was wrong with that?

Never underestimate what you can do or who you can become.

My third rule: ignore the naysayers

It is quite natural to have big dreams and big goals and to share them with others – who will say "Keep on dreaming, it will never happen", or "You are not intelligent enough to get there", or "You are a poor girl".

It started when I was only 16. I said I wanted to be the next Oprah Winfrey, I wanted to transform lives. The immediate response was, "Are you out of your mind? You have to be a millionaire to be known internationally and to transform lives!"

Touching lives globally has nothing to do with being a millionaire: forget about it. I said, "I want to be like Oprah Winfrey, a successful woman who transforms lives, I want to be like John C Maxwell, the number one leadership guru in the world."

When I told my friends, my colleagues, my managers, their reaction was – "Sally, you make me laugh, you should become a comedian!" They said, "Let's see, you are an administrative assistant, you work for the minimum wage, how are you going to make this become a reality?" "No one will ever listen to you – remember you are from Laventille, and nothing good comes out of Laventille." Everywhere I turned, I was laughed at and faced with negativity.

Luckily, I did not listen. I began to make greater investments in myself. I became self-taught in many areas; I purchased books upon books on leadership, personal development, building confidence, speaking in public, empowering others. I took classes upon classes. I began to mentor my co-workers, my students; I gave free career guidance, I began to read the *Harvard Business Review.* I sacrificed fun to spend time reading and learning.

I became a passionate eater ... I hungered for knowledge and ate it with a passion. Then suddenly I stumbled upon *A Minute with Maxwell* and my life was changed forever. I enrolled in The John Maxwell University where I was coached by the best on how to become my best and give of my best using the John Maxwell approach.

Finally, I got what I always wanted. But you know what was interesting? If I had not believed in who I was and what I could become, if I had allowed my situation and limiting beliefs to deter me, if I had allowed the naysayers to have their way, I would never have been who I am today. The naysayers and my environment simply fueled my energy to become better and fight harder.

Remain focused, and do not let your environment, the circumstances of your family life, or the naysayers, deter you from achieving your goal.

The fourth rule: be persistent and work, work, work

You have to be persistent and don't give up. *No pain no gain.*

When I joined The John Maxwell University, I was coached for an hour at 2am every Tuesday. From 11pm to 3am on other days I studied. From 7am to 3pm I worked in an organization, and I devoted 4pm to 9pm to my doctorate.

You have to be persistent and work, work, work, no matter what happens. WORK, WORK, WORK. Be PERSISTENT and you will get there.

My fifth and last rule: don't just take, give something back

Take the focus off yourself and you will see the billions of people who need your help. Become a servant-leader: serve your people. Every opportunity I have, I try to give something back to society.

There are many people who are less fortunate than you are, and no matter how small your contribution, it can make a big difference in their lives.

Change your world and the world around you will change.

SEVENTEEN

Boundaries:
When Do I Say No?

> *"Love is when the hearts of two friends become one. It is caring, understanding, sharing, forgiving, respect and mutual confidence. It is integrity and loyalty through the good and bad times. It is seeing beyond their imperfections."* - **Sally Ann Bharat**

"**S**WEETHEART, YOU HAVE GAINED WEIGHT, are you overeating?" Jack asks his girlfriend.

Janice quickly responds: "No! The medication has contributed significantly to my weight gain. I am exercising and watching my diet."

Jack, sarcastically: "Yeah right, you should not be eating any food at all, you are a pig, and you probably eat all day and all night."

When do you say no to this form of abuse, or any type of abuse? Quite often, it's difficult to walk away. It's difficult to say NO to verbal, physical and emotional abuse, or even to set boundaries. We try to be people-pleasers because we lack confidence in ourselves. We let limiting beliefs about who we are or what we can achieve control us.

But saying NO can be a turning point in your life. Saying NO can be the solution to the problems you encounter. We need to have confidence in who we are and be able to set boundaries. We need to be able to say NO to situations that contradict our beliefs and values.

Often when we say YES to everything, we are basically telling our partners that we stand for nothing and fall for everything. We have no boundaries, so we will accept whatever is hurled at us.

But this is a lie we have chosen to believe. You have a choice in every situation. And if a bad choice is made, STOP, recalibrate, and make another choice – otherwise a choice will be made for you. Most of the time, we say yes because we want to be loved or liked by our partners. But this can take you down a road filled with abuse, stress and – even worse – death.

Here are some tips to consider.

Walk away

Once under an abuser's influence and control, you begin to accept things in the relationship that you would never otherwise tolerate. You desperately seek validation from a person, and you make changes in your life to accommodate them. Changes like the way you wear your hair, the way you dress, putting on clothes that were never your style. You indulge in things that are not of your stature.

This is not entirely bad, because in a relationship you do want to make sure you look attractive, thinking of how your companion would like to see you.

It becomes a problem when you are running around trying to do everything you can for someone who does nothing for you – and perhaps you are not even worth a compliment.

Would you believe me if I told you that an abuser can break you down to the point where they can do you wrong and then tell you that you don't have a right to be angry? And you will believe it because they have made you think *you* are lucky they are even with you.

What do you do at this point?

Take a long look in the mirror and recognize how beautiful you are. When you can see clearly how beautiful you are, then you can begin to love yourself, and no one can take that away.

Love yourself enough to walk away.

Tune into your inner sense of yes and no

Sarri Gilman, MA, MFT, a psychotherapist and author of *Transform Your Boundaries*, suggests that we think of our boundaries through the metaphor of an inner compass with two words written on it: *Yes* and *No*.

We all have an inner sense of wisdom, which tells us when something is a yes or a no. The problem arises when we ignore or argue with that inner voice.

If you are not used to tuning into your intuition, practice paying attention to how you are feeling. Using tools such as meditation and mindfulness is one way to tune in to your thoughts and feelings in the moment.

Learn how to tolerate the reactions of others

"Boundary setting will unleash emotions," Gilman says, "when you listen to your own yes and no." Other people may get angry or disappointed. The reality is that whenever you set boundaries with people, their reaction may not be pleasant. But you can still maintain the boundaries that you have set.

Engage in acts of compassionate self-care

You may have heard the popular saying, "You can't pour from an empty cup." If you want to be giving and compassionate toward others, it is critical that you apply the same compassion towards yourself.

You deserve to treat yourself with the same kindness and compassion that you give to others. Set aside some weekly time for acts of self-care, which can help you relax, recharge, and connect with yourself.

EIGHTEEN

Valuing Your Organization's Most Valuable Asset

MAGINE ARRIVING AT THE OFFICE only to discover that the desktop computer and all the confidential files are missing. Immediately you will:

- o contact your supervisor and security manager
- o launch an investigation to determine who and what is responsible
- o develop a plan to ensure that such a loss doesn't recur.

Now, would you do the same thing if one of your organization's highly skilled employees (its most valuable asset) was poached by the competition, or just walked out of the door? Would you launch an investigation? Identify the root causes? Develop a contingency plan to prevent a recurrence? Probably not!

It is essential to understand that employees are an organization's most valuable asset. Simple but necessary actions by management, such as giving recognition for hard work, maintaining open lines of two-way communication, and being transparent about where the organization is headed, are just a few ways to keep your employees happy and your turnover rate low. Taking these simple tasks for granted can leave employees feeling undervalued and ready to call it quits.

Here are some of the best strategies you can implement to improve employee retention at your own organization.

Leverage the manager-employee relationship

Managers who can determine the needs of their employees and find quick solutions to employee problems are seen as motivators by employees. Organizations can leverage this type of employee relationship to build trust, to have maximum influence on employees, and to increase the productivity levels of a firm. If managers are unable to build a successful relationship with employees, it can have a negative effect and result in demotivation and a decline in performance.

Revitalize the job

It's common for people with solid potential to suffer discontent and yet to stay on the job. Rather than leaving, employees find ways to disengage, and their departure is psychological rather than physical. This is sometimes referred to as "retiring in place."

Such disengagement can be just as costly as real departure. Plausible approaches to this challenge include combining tasks, forming self-directed teams, increasing contact with clients, rotating assignments, and job sharing.

Avoid micromanaging

Why micromanage when you are employing talented individuals? Managers should be able to demonstrate trust in the capabilities of their employees. Allowing employees to take on new projects they have no experience in promotes growth and encourages them to take initiatives.

In other words, give employees the opportunity to showcase their excellence. When assigning tasks, let them express their creativity and empower them to make decisions for which they will be held accountable.

In my organization, I want employees to take risks and try new things. If they succeed, then they have experience to add to their resume. If they fail, then they learn.

Check in regularly

Giving employees the opportunity to discuss their strengths, career aspirations, and the items they struggle with, will show your workforce that you are dedicated to their professional growth as well as to addressing their concerns.

Weed out toxic employees

They may be well paid, receive recognition, and have opportunities to grow, but people will leave if they dislike their supervisor.

Paedro was a training assistant working for a globally recognized organization. Although he enjoyed his job and was well paid, his new boss was the type that revels in tyranny, was perceived as incompetent, and took credit for all Paedro's hard work. Nine months later, Paedro made the decision to quit his job, after working with the company for 15 years, because of his dislike for his boss. Two months later, the boss was fired.

Organizations need to be crystal clear about what they will and will not tolerate. What do toxic employees do? They intimidate, condescend or demean, swear, behave rudely, belittle people in front of others, give only negative feedback, lie, act in a sexist or racist way, withhold critical information, blow up in meetings, refuse to accept blame or accountability, gossip and spread rumors, use fear as a motivator, etc. Such behaviors do not foster respect, trust, or good performance.

Inject fun into the workplace

Studies have shown that fun enhances creativity – and it certainly does not diminish productivity when everyone's work and collaboration goals are clear. Consider simple activities such as frequent contests, celebrations, and team-building activities. Be creative. Sometimes, in a negative situation, it is important to rediscover humor. When employees can laugh in the face of an impending deadline, for example, they can diffuse a lot of tension and stress.

NINETEEN

Appreciation & Gratitude

I MAGINE THIS. *It is Friday, the last day of the work week, you are tired and don't feel like going to work, but you decide to go in anyway. As you enter the workplace, you are greeted by a beautiful little princess and offered a buffet breakfast.*

What immediate feelings would you have if this happened? This simple act of appreciation shown to you by your organization would be a wonderful way of saying thank you.

Employee recognition is the timely, informal or formal acknowledgement of a person's or team's behavior, effort or business result that supports the organization's goals and values, and which has clearly gone beyond normal expectations.

On the surface level, appreciation is good for employee engagement, motivation and retention. Employee appreciation and recognition create a unique company culture and strengthen employee relationships.

The psychological effects of workplace appreciation and gratitude

1) Showing gratitude to your employees creates a friendly work environment. When employees and their work are valued, their satisfaction and productivity increase and they are motivated to maintain their good work. Overall, employee appreciation not only boosts performance and engagement but has the added bonus of improving the employee's well-being and health.

2) Showing appreciation or gratitude to co-workers creates more social and prosocial interaction. According to an article generated by *The Positive Psychology Program*, "People who participated in gratitude exercises were found to be more prosocial than others." The article defines prosocial as "promoting others' well-being usually through altruistic acts." When gratitude is embedded in company culture, employees are more willing to share their positive feelings with others, whether by helping out with a project or taking time to notice and recognize those who have gone the extra mile.

3) Increased individual productivity is another valuable effect. The act of recognizing desired behavior encourages the repetition of that behavior, which in turn increases productivity by a process of positive reinforcement. This is classic behavioral psychology. The reinforced behavior

supports the organization's mission and key performance indicators.

4) Greater employee satisfaction and enjoyment of work leads to more time spent focusing on the job and less time complaining.

5) The organization receives higher loyalty and satisfaction scores from customers.

6) Teamwork between employees is enhanced.

7) Retention of quality employees improves, with lower employee turnover.

8) There are fewer negative effects such as absenteeism and stress.

9) Lastly, the greatest effect of appreciation and gratitude is that happiness and other emotions are immediately felt, whether we are the ones expressing or receiving gratitude.

Gratitude creates good feelings, cheerful memories, and better self-esteem; it enhances relaxation and optimism. These feelings create a pay-it- forward and *we're in this together* mentality in the workplace, which in turn makes your organization more successful.

Twenty

Planning For the Unknown
Succession Planning

HAT WOULD YOU DO in your organization if a key employee resigned, fell ill, or had to be fired tomorrow? Would you be prepared?

In recent months, a number of government offices and private sector organizations have had significant job cuts, resulting in a number of key personnel losing their jobs. Neither government offices nor private sector organizations have demonstrated that a strategic approach to succession planning was in place.

Finding the right person to run an organization or ministry can be a great challenge. But without a well-groomed candidate, a change of leadership can have an adverse effect on an organization, especially if the departure is sudden.

Proper succession planning acknowledges that key staff will not be with an organization indefinitely. It therefore provides a plan and process for addressing the changes that will occur when they leave. While most succession planning focuses on the most senior manager, the executive director, all key positions should be included in the plan. These can be defined as positions that are crucial to the operation of the organization. People who hold senior positions or who have many years of experience will, logically, be difficult to replace.

Four secrets of succession planning

Four "best practice" procedures are commonly used by organizations.

Analysis

The first focuses on the development of a solid understanding of the most significant challenges the organization and its industry are likely to face over the next four to six years, and the skills and experiences the chief executive will need to lead the company past those hurdles.

Directors must fight the tendency to think the answer is to find a younger version of the incumbent CEO or of other key personnel.

For example, Trinidad and Tobago is experiencing a deep recession. The oil and gas industry has contracted, and that has had a ripple effect on many organizations in both the public and private sectors.

In the case of the helicopter companies, for example, those in leadership positions will need to consider how to replace key skilled members of staff such as pilots, engineers, quality managers, and directors. Only in the rarest cases will future challenges require the same skills that worked in the past.

Thus, investing in a credible forecast about the future makes it possible to understand the skills and capabilities a CEO or key personnel will need.

Development

Development begins with the identification of a small number of people who could be made ready in two to four years. A great deal can be done in that time to develop an executive, whether it involves rotations in different functional areas, international assignments, or something else.

A caution regarding internal candidates: if succession planning is not carefully timed, candidates will be either too quick or too slow to develop; those ready too soon become targets for head-hunters, while those not yet ready are of little use.

Selection

As the transition approaches, the internal candidates should be ready. The scanning for external candidates should be updated. The best selection practice involves inviting all internal candidates to give presentations to the board, in which they describe their vision for the company's next five years. After a presentation and discussion, the likelihood is – if the development of internal talent has been successful – that a clear winner will be revealed. If none emerges, then it is time for the board to consider external candidates.

Transition

In the case of a CEO, a best-practice transition focuses on both the on-boarding process (i.e. getting up to speed with the job) and the first 12 months of a new CEO's tenure.

Internal and external successors experience on-boarding differently, but a critical presumption is that before the successor's first day, the board has made certain that he or she has begun to develop relationships with board members, has had sufficient time with the outgoing CEO to complete appropriate hand-offs, and has a sense of which areas require immediate action.

EPILOGUE

*P*eople often ask me how I discovered the secret to personal and professional success that allowed me to grow in the midst of the office politics and adversity. Were these principles based on my personal experiences? Where did I discover my principles? Certainly I've learned much from studying good leadership styles, the attitudes and behaviors of people in a work environment and I've also learned humility, the spirit of learning. I've read many great books. I've interviewed many leaders who were ahead of me. And I've learned a great deal not only from my personal experiences but from the experiences of others within and outside of the work environment. But the greatest lessons I learned came from John C Maxwell's personal growth and development books. And I think his teachings on the 15 Invaluable Laws of Growth and Sometimes You Win, Sometimes You Learn will be an encouragement to you.

LEARNING TO GROW YOURSELF

"You have the power to align yourself with the best, whose presence will call forth your best" **Sally Ann Bharat**

One of the greatest investments you can make is in yourself and to grow yourself, you must first know yourself. Becoming intentional about your personal growth and development helps you overcome many obstacles both personally and professionally.

In fact, you become self-aware and learn the skills of self-management which in turn helps you to become resilient and have the ability to overcome many challenges life will toss at you.

HAVING A WINNING MIND-SET AND ATTITUDE

"Determination helps you discover new possibilities, create new opportunities, that brings a diversion from all distraction until you've reached your destination" **Sally Ann Bharat**

We often think that success was handed over to the top performers and successful leaders. That wasn't the case. In order to succeed in any area of your life, you must work twice as hard to achieve success. It's a slow grind. And it starts with your mind-set and attitude. You have to build a winning mind-set and develop a winning attitude in order to achieve success. According to John C Maxwell, "People with a lot of talent often perform at a high level, but the greatest – the absolute best of the best – achieve the highest heights because they possess the spirit of learning. To have a winning mind-set and winning attitude, you must be willing to have a spirit of learning.

START WINNING TODAY!

*"You will encounter many DEFEATS in life and significant Growth in the process. But you must NEVER be DEFEATED or remain STAGNANT. When you encounter defeats, you DISCOVER who you are and how RESILIENT you are." **Sally Ann Bharat***

Do you believe you were born to win, to be confident, and to believe in yourself? Whatever is in you can be your secret to success both personally and professionally. You have the choice to grow yourself in the midst of adversity and be the best YOU that YOU can be. And you can develop a Make It Happen Attitude. So start winning today. Embrace the winning principles. Start believing in yourself, having the confidence in you, to know that you can overcome any situation faced with at the office. Remember, your key to success is a winning mind-set, winning attitude and a learning spirit.

"Born To Win – Be Confident, Believe in YOU!"

SALLY ANN BHARAT